CW00551090

THE ROOM THAT CHANGES YOUR BRAIN

Cell-rejuvenating
architecture and design

by Rosalyn Dexter

Published by Outside the Bigger Box
www.outsidethebiggerbox.com

Text © Rosalyn Dexter 2013
Design & layout: Rosalyn Dexter

ISBN 978-0-9927836-0-0

Production: Blacker Limited
(www.blackerdesign.co.uk)

THE ROOM THAT CHANGES YOUR BRAIN

A journey into the mind

revealing the power of design

to shape our lives

Many people inspired and supported me over the years in the writing of this book. To name a few would be to overlook the many.

Thank you with appreciation and love.

Contents

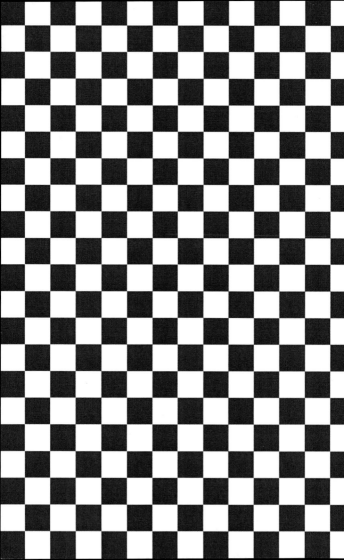

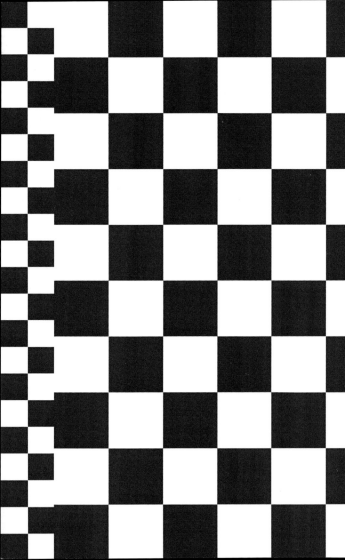

Chapter 1
Story

This is a small book that tells a big story: a story of cell-rejuvenating design, distilled from research that has emerged over the last three decades. Packed with groundbreaking evidence, it will change our view of design.

The information has been collated from the research of the finest minds in neuroscience, psychology, neurophysics and epigenetics, it offers evidence that, when woven together, builds a radical new approach for design. It will change our perception of reality and our understanding of the power of design to shape our lives.

I dedicate this to two particular individuals who influenced me; the celebrated architect of the 1920s, Richard Neutra, who cared deeply about design and the people it sheltered. His early ideas encouraged my sentiment for architecture and design to be meaningful. The other, my father, an eccentric who lived out of a suitcase most of his life and didn't give a jot for design. Early on, he encouraged me to develop a healthy scepticism in relation to the extravagance of design as a surface embellishment in a troubled world.

My father's dismissive views on design were seeded during the 1920s and 30s in a Vienna, whose beauty he found contrasted violently with its politics. Both he and Neutra shared this city as their birthplace and its centres of excellence for their different fields of study.

Vienna was of particular significance to me because it was from here, that research emerged to shine a light from an unexpected angle on the subject matter that unfolds here.

The journey.

Most of us recognize that we are influenced in our choices by our life experience. My father's views resulted in him not supporting my studies in design. This was fortuitous, for it meant I had to pay my own way through college. He was an eye specialist and to fund my studies while at art school, I trained as a dispensing optician. This later led me to investigate how we see with our imagination – and on to the field of neuroscience. It was neuroscience that informed me about the role of the imagination in cell-rejuvenating architecture and design.

My desire to enter the arena of design developed in my early years. By the time I was 12 years old I had lived in 30 homes on land and many cabins at sea, while attending over 24 schools around the globe, in tow to my peripatetic father. In my young adult years, having settled in England, I began my studies in fine art, completed my thesis on architecture, and never looked back.

I went on to develop a successful design company creating luxury lifestyle buildings. But the memory of my father's scepticism goaded me over the years to seek something meaningful within design.

What I found unfolds in these chapters.

2
Rejuvenation by design

It was back in the 1920s that Richard Neutra first suggested we become more aware of how our psyche works when it comes to design. Half a century later, we had conclusive evidence of the profound influence of the environment at the psychological and neurological level. But we didn't take it on board to any major degree. Another decade on from that, in the late 1970s, an experiment at Harvard unveiled what Neutra never anticipated, that – due to how we function neurologically – a room's design could regenerate our cells and even trigger cellular rejuvenation. Again we ignored it. Even when three decades on from that, in 2010, the Harvard trial was replicated with phenomenal results – we continued to ignore the evidence.

I was curious about the evidence and our resistance to it, especially in light of the positive results... until I came across some research by eminent neuroscientist Professor Erik Kandel, in which he proposed that we resist the new until it becomes familiar.

The plan here then, is to make this information familiar by unpacking sufficient supporting evidence from diverse fields, to reveal the neurologically transformative and hypnotic influence of design.

Once this information becomes familiar, cell-rejuvenating regenerating architecture and design can become part of our daily life.

With that in mind, as the first few chapters unfold, we will be introduced to vision and our senses in general. We will touch on the source of our imagination and inspiration, cognitive psychology, and how feelings and reason weave together our sense of meaning and our personal experience of reality. This leads us to the middle chapters where we unveil the surreal reality that science has proven we are a part of. For this we touch on consciousness, the particle field, how time is subjective and rejuvenation is possible; as well as the neurological influence of colour, shape and form. After this we look at the tricks of the mind and how they can be harnessed.

Then we are on the road home, unveiling the power of language to frame image and story in architecture and design, as well as looking at branding in relation to buildings and our herding instincts. In the last chapters we take a glance towards epigenetics and its ground-breaking evidence on how our environment affects our gene expression.

We are then on our way to creating the kind of strategic design that can actively, positively manipulate us at the cellular level.

☐ ☐

Our resistance over the years to acknowledging the evidence on the power of our environment is a curious thing, yet there are some like Neutra who insightfully embraced the possibility long before Kandel's evidence helped explain it. I was invited to consult at Downing St a few years ago where, having discussed views on the potential of the design and mind concepts I was researching, I was asked what Winston Churchill may have said about the direction of my work. Rather serendipitously, while sitting in his famous armchair, I was able to quote the great man himself.

He had said – 'we shape our buildings thereafter they shape us'.

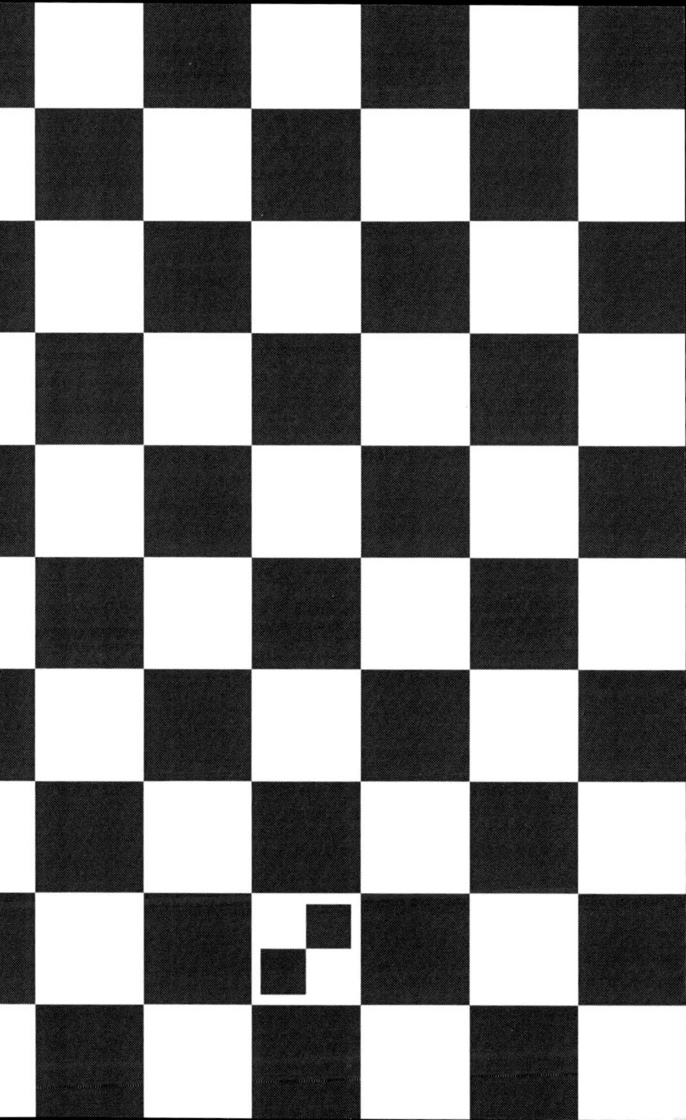

3
Renew again and again…

I recognize that the idea of cell-rejuvenating architecture and design can sound somewhat surreal, but as I said there have been clues going back decades. It was in 1979 at Harvard that Professor Ellen Langer executed a study that is just turning up on our radar today.

She and her team manipulated an environment for a group of geriatrics, where the overall experience was set up to focus the participant's thoughts and feelings on their younger years. Memorabilia was used to induce and reinforce nostalgia in many forms. In the building itself, the attire, the television programmes they watched, the radio programmes they listened to, their conversations and the décor – all of these were from earlier decades, a time when the participants would have been 20 years younger. By the end of just one week, for the majority, their visual thresholds had reversed and there was improved cognitive ability and IQ. Most had enhanced manual dexterity and were moving with more pace. Some even discarding walking sticks. Their systems weren't just regenerating with cells replenishing – they were renewing their otherwise presumed to be atrophying cells. They were rejuvenating.

As a trial, it was a phenomenon but without the technology we have today to measure brain activity, there was nowhere to go except to await supporting evidence. This has since come and unfolds in these pages.

□ □

In 1986, a few years after the Harvard trial, Professor Roger Ulrich of Pennsylvania University recorded improved recovery time for patients in a hospital ward with a window, compared to a ward without a window. There was an improved recovery rate of 20%; along with a phenomenal 60% reduction in analgesic requirement. This was not a behaviourally influenced study as at Harvard, there were no mind games going on. At this time, still lacking the benefit of current technology such as fMRi's to measure brain function, the source of the neurobiochemical acceleration remained a mystery. As with the Harvard trial, science had to wait for corroborating evidence. By necessity, the accrual of scientific evidence is at a slow burn: verifying detail takes time. The evidence, though, has since come.

It seems – we do shape our buildings – and there after they do shape us

Part of what science confirmed as we turned into this new millennium is that our brain is neuroplastic. What this means is that our neurons – the nerve cells in the brain – renew and reorganize, increasing and decreasing in number in response to input. This they do until we die. Quite a different view to last century when it was thought that our brain cells, our neurons, stopped developing in adulthood.

Our neurons operate by generating an electrical charge that diffuses as electrochemical signals throughout our system; strengthening some connections between neurons and weakening others. Change happens as neurons that fire together wire together and neurons that fire apart, wire apart – transforming our biochemistry.

Before I explain how our neuroplastic brain, the firing of neurons and the strategic design of our personal environment can accelerate recovery and trigger rejuvenation, let me explain something about how we see. For our day-to-day process of observation, is critical to this neurobiochemical phenomenon.

Neuroscientists Irving Biederman and Edward Vessel, when looking into aesthetics in 2006, unveiled a study that had been overlooked 25 years before. It revealed there is an increase in density of mu-opioid receptors along the visual pathway, these reeptors trigger the release of opiate-like substances. Our visual pathway lies between the association cortex of our brain, that interprets what we see, and our eye's mechanics for perspective. The receptors act as binding sites for endorphins such as serotonin and dopamine. Dopamine is generally considered the molecule of addiction – giving us a charge like some experience with cocaine – and serotonin is known to alter our mood. So, opiate-like substances that influence a pleasure response are triggered along our visual pathway, influencing our interpretation of our surroundings. With this and the process of vision involving a level of feeling, reasoning and interpretation, I use the term perception when it comes to vision.

These opiate like substances affect how we perceive what we see, and even influence our biological clock and sense of time. With these triggers influencing our perception, what we each 'see' is not necessarily what is literally out there. What we perceive is our interpretation woven with our personal imagination; fed by our history, experiences, culture and more. Add to this that there are more neural connections running from our emotional centre – which is our lymbic system, to the neocortex – the part of the brain responsible for the evolution of our intelligence, than there are coming from it as reasoning centre; and we find what science has 'officially confirmed', that feelings are primary to reason. We have a feeling-led influence contributing to our 'reasoned' interpretation of what we 'imagine' we perceive.

I say 'imagine' what we perceive, because with something as basic as perception involving a reasoning, feeling function and opiate like triggers, we will find we are designed to integrate our imagination into what we see. That we integrate imagination into our interpretation may not sound all that outrageous but the ramifications are. I mentioned that my early studies into vision led me to investigate how we see with our imagination. Due to the process of neuroplasticity, whereby our cells ever renew and reorganize in response to input, we find that we respond at the cellular level to our interpretation of what we perceive.

If we respond to what we see and what we see is woven with what we imagine, then at the cellular level we are changing in response to what we imagine.

Let me repeat this.

Not only do our cells change, renew and reorganize until we die, increasing and decreasing in number, but this change is influenced by what we imagine.

Those geriatrics at Harvard rejuvenated their cells in response to the surrounding narrative – being elderly set no limit. With the hospital window, something of interpretation and imagination accelerated the recovery of those patients.

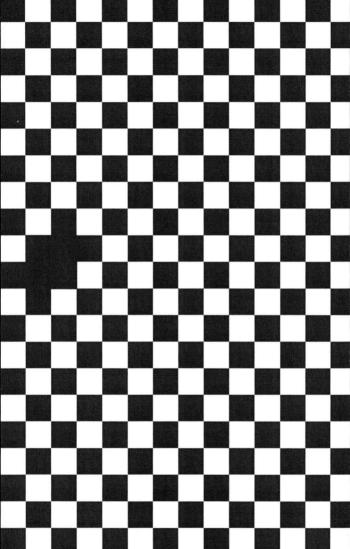

4
Perceiving the new

Back in 1910 Richard Neutra was studying the work of the psychologist Wilhelm Wundt. Considered the father of modern psychology, Wundt had identified that both eye movement and head movement are inseparable; he found that the muscles around the eye are connected to the muscles of the head. Decades later in 1976, a study was done at the Langley Porter Neuropsychiatric Institute in San Francisco on the correlation of eye movements with neurophysiological processes. There it was found that eye movements were related to specific cognitive processes. Eyes moving up and left triggers memory – like the colour of ones car, whereas eyes moving up and right is for imagination – such as imagining our room painted a new colour. Eyes moving laterally left, for an auditory response – as in remembering our favourite tune. And so on. Generally our eyes move in the opposite direction for left handed people.

Where at Langley they found that a movement of the eye could affect neurological processes and Wundt identified that a movement of the eyes and head are inseparable, I noted from other studies an additional and rather surreal connection. We are touching on time and cell rejuvenation here and how our environment and experience of it can stimulate that. Well, it seems a movement of the head can affect our reference to linear time. Using a simple thought exercise; if we look upward, physiologically it is harder to think of the past. If we look down it is harder to think of the future – compared to looking upward. Try it. A manoeuvre of the head and eyeline is changing our flow of thoughts on a spacial time line.

In studying Wundt's ideas along with other research, Neutra was focused on how we think, perceive and transform information while in our environments; that which today would be called the cognitive processes.

□ □

Alongside Frank Lloyd Wright, Neutra was a celebrated architect in his time, best known for his international modernist style. What he was less well known for were his developing ideas that today would be recognized as core to cognitive psychology. He, of course, hadn't forseen that imagination could affect us physiologically as well as psychologically. It is only today that we have the privilege of technology that can record the previously immeasurable responses of the brain to stimuli, including imagination. We now even know its portal, it is the anterior superior temporal gyrus.

□ □

We know more about the brain than ever before. We can measure the influence and source of feelings, the impact of language and how symbols register. We recognize which parts of the brain are used to identify form, texture, contour, density, mass and proportion. We even know the areas that interpret buildings and preferred locations.

The mechanism of vision involves more than we have generally understood, for we see with our interpretative brain. This may seem like an obvious statement, yet most of us tend to assume that the eyes are the window via which we perceive what is actually surrounding us; rather than seeing what we 'rationally imagine' and reason with our brain as observer. In seeing with the brain, we each bring our history and reasoning with us; differentiating our personal interpretation from everyone else. The result is that we assume our view on the reality we perceive is the same for everyone… and the 'real' one.

Whatever it is we each see; what we do know is that cells ever renew and reorganize in response to what we imagine. This offers a clue to what may have happened for the participants at Harvard; an experience that resulted in rejuvenation at the cellular level.

☐ ☐

The following question arises: if rejuvenation was trig-gered for the geriatrics at Harvard, as their imagination, reasoning and feelings interpreted the retro/reminiscing experience, could we influence our system prescriptively at the cellular level? If we are strategic and plant meaning-ful associations in the design of our environment, will our system respond in accordance with our interpretation while there? Though even as I ask this, I must mention that we of course do not change willy nilly. For those geriatrics the resulting rejuvenation was not so simple as incubating in some general environment where they could reminisce. Their systems neurologically bought into the experience; deliberately set up for them to do so.

There are protective mechanisms in place – and thank goodness. We wouldn't want to change in response to just any input; otherwise the experience for medical staff in an intensive care ward, as an example, would be untenable. We have to 'buy into' the narrative of our surroundings at the neurobiological level. There has to be context, mean-ing and relevance for change to happen; a relevance whereby it is pertinent to our circumstance.

What we are finding is that our room and its narrative becomes an extension of our neural system. We may be willing to accept the eyes as an extension of the brain but there may be a resistance to the idea that a room can be an extension of our brain. Certainly we know we do not change in response to all input, but we do inhabit an easily hypnotized system. This was illustrated not only by the Harvard trial decades ago, but more recently when the trial was replicated by the BBC in 'The Young Ones', a primetime documentary series in 2010.

Professor Langer's original research had just been published as a book, and the programme followed the guidelines of that and her original study. The geriatric participants this time were a group of elderly celebrities and the results were again phenomenal. The majority doubled their stamina and manual dexterity; memory was enhanced and visual thresholds reversed, improving their vision. Some discarded their walking sticks, all within a week; witnessed by millions on camera.

So, why haven't most of us heard about this? Why aren't the documentary and its results all over the press and why aren't we actively seeking its clues for our own environment? One would think with our personal quest for a revitalizing elixir and the amount spent on the promise of youth with creams, potions and cosmetic surgery, that at least by

2010 when they broadcast this documentary, we would have taken note. One would think that we would have grasped the evident promise of rejuvenating cellular change via design. After all, design in our environment is something we can all access. Yet, despite the programme being broadcast to millions, even by autumn 2013 there was hardly any editorial; this even though the tabloids are quick to report if a celebrity looks suspiciously wrinkle free.

Curious isn't it, that celebrities rejuvenating naturally via a purposely manipulated environment didn't take up substantial column inches? Back then and now.

□ □

In part it is because we have that inbuilt resistance to the 'new', as Kandel proposed. If it requires a change to our core beliefs, we resist. Our assumptions on atrophy run deep and this evidence required a change to those.

Professor Kandel received his Nobel prize in 2005 for research on memory and learning. He had identified that there is a need for information to become familiar before we can relate to it as ordinary; if we don't relate to it 'as ordinary', we can pass it by. With the BBC programme, we passed it by.

One of the problems with the programme was that the producers didn't offer diverse evidence on how we function in order to support and reinforce what was otherwise less familiar to us – the viewer. Such evidence might have helped us digest the otherwise seemingly outrageous information – garnering a familiarity with it is key. The BBC programme only offered isolated information that went against old reasoning we have bought into over the years on ageing. We ignored it.

Here we will unpack information from diverse fields in support of a new approach to design, towards it becoming familiar.

5
We pass by time

Neutra had been curious about Wundt's work on head and eye movements and their interconnections. He had also studied a form of occular phenomenology.

Phenomenology in terms of perception is a philosophy about sensations and images existing via the meaning they exhibit to the observer. The celebrated philosopher of phenomenology, Maurice Merleau-Ponty, who wrote *The Phenomenology of Perception*, was actively engaged with psychology and the cognitive sciences; he proposed that that which is perceived cannot be disentangled from the body.

□ □

Phenomenology as a way of informing our experience was a route for Neutra in the absence of scientific evidence.

Though I found much of the literature on phenomenology written in complex theoretical terms, I sensed that it could touch the abstract experience of architecture in a constructive way. Aiding an understanding of some of the contemporary evidence emerging in the neurological, biological and cognitive sciences, where the research related to the impact of our environment.

Research into neuroscience and other disciplines was not as easily accessible to a non-scientist like myself a couple of decades ago; the internet was only just emerging into common use. So investigating the philosophical route of phenomenology, parallax and the haptic realm helped.

Parallax, in simple terms, is the effect of moving through a building and its changing perspectives. The horizontal and vertical lines and shapes created by the ceilings, floors and walls as we move through, manoeuvrering in and out of our visual field, and our experience and response corporeally and as an observer. The haptic realm is mostly about touch, though it also feeds into balance and positional awareness.

All of these influence our sensorial spacial experience in our environment.

If looking up inhibits our ability to think on the past, and opiate-like substances are triggered along our visual pathway affecting our mood and sense of time; what happens in a building that causes us to look up as we move through? And what if we find the building beautiful. For scientists have found beauty triggers endorphins and affects our biological clock?

Time is far more subjective than we generally suppose.

As regards the role of cognition, I did wonder why it is still not particularly emphasized in design. Comparatively few architecture PHDs refer to it or to Wundt's work, despite often referencing Neutra. The eager young minds of architecture today reflect with great enthusiasm on phenomenology; it is almost as if when it comes to reflecting on room as more than shelter, the poetry of philosophy is preferred to the science of cognition. Neuroscience is developing a dialogue at some universities, but this is mostly with reference to aesthetics and art. In some ways cognitive psychology is almost as separate from architecture today as it was 100 years ago… despite the evidence.

We find this with the general perception of Neutra. Though he had written books and won prizes, his particular interest on the psyche in architecture is mostly overlooked. This despite it being Lovell's now famous Health House, completed in 1928, that put Neutra on the celebrity map and the cover of *Time* Magazine. Lovell commissioned him as architect for all the benefits he recognised he would bring to it, a bias now mostly passed by. Note the name – 'Health House'.

The 'Health House', 1928

I was curious, was Neutra's interest in the psyche being overlooked, tied in with Kandel's findings on our resistance to the new and the need for information to become familiar before we can embrace it?

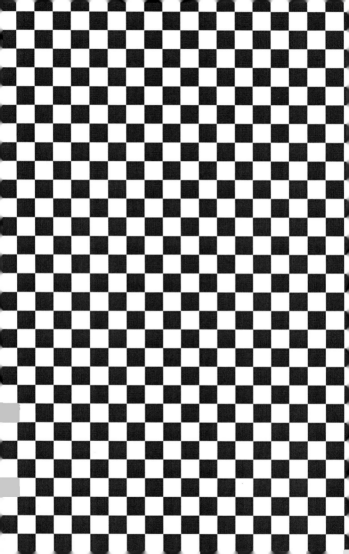

Today we understand more of how our system works and are finding design to be neurologically hypnotic. Lingering in a room woven with a deliberate narrative, where the associations are sourced from deep contextual references, our system changes in accordance with our interpretation of the messages embedded there. Fed by imagination and led by feelings, our neuroplastic system continually inter-prets and responds.

Here we deepen our awareness of the processes involved in creating that neurological response, so that we may be more strategic with how we weave our own design.

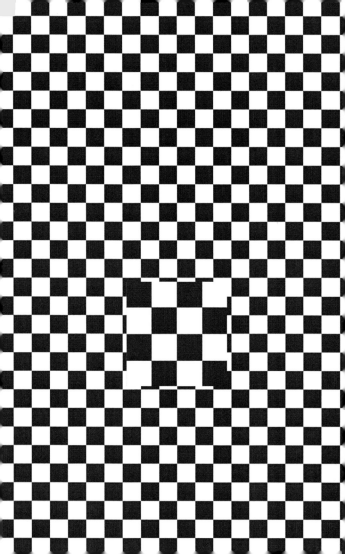

6
Change happens

With emerging knowledge, we can approach our environment and its potential in a more informed manner than last century. When it comes to neurology, we can measure responses in the brain like never before – we can even measure our response to meaning, thoughts and feelings. We have learnt which parts of the brain respond to symbols. We even know that curves inhibit stress hormones and are finding that angles excite them; different shapes trigger different chemical responses and colour and texture further influence those. Our system and its cells are primed to respond to the details of our surroundings as a cell in a petri dish does to its environment. We inhabit a highly responsive mind/body system and where cells ever reorganize and renew – we don't just respond, we change. We just haven't generally understood the process of such change – nor that our environment could impact us so profoundly.

Having long accepted that a cell responds to its environment, we just need to begin to think of ourselves as a living structure of over 50 trillion thinking, feeling, reasoning, associating cells that respond to our environment. Our space becomes a mega petri dish with us as an extension of it and it of us. Its form, curves and angles woven with meaning, trigger the firing of neurons, affecting our development as our feedback system feeds back ad infinitum. Our environment becomes not so much a shelter like a shell for a snail but more a chrysalis for our inner butterfly.

There are of course generic influences where – for example – blue can lower our temperature and high ceilings enhance our creativity. However, calculated meaning-filled design can trigger a whole other cascade of change – the knowledge of which creates a new conversation in the field of design.

A zeitgeist is upon us.

With what we now know, designing our environments without an understanding of their transformative potential is meaningless. However much a fan of style and innovation we may be, we need to awaken to what science is unveiling. Even beauty, though subjective, can enhance the immune system, affect our biological clock and raise our pain threshold. So, let us more consciously bring a sense of beauty into our environment, especially if it affects our pain threshold, our tolerance. We can all do with more of that.

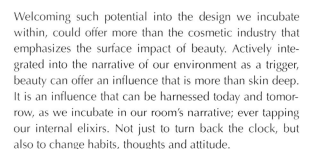

Welcoming such potential into the design we incubate within, could offer more than the cosmetic industry that emphasizes the surface impact of beauty. Actively integrated into the narrative of our environment as a trigger, beauty can offer an influence that is more than skin deep. It is an influence that can be harnessed today and tomorrow, as we incubate in our room's narrative; ever tapping our internal elixirs. Not just to turn back the clock, but also to change habits, thoughts and attitude.

I realize we may be willing to buy into the idea of good design affecting how we feel but to propose that it contributes to rejuvenation, the changing of habits, behaviours and how we think – may seem rather ambitious.

□ □

Biologists did a study a while back in which it was found that an ordinary green locust becomes a gregarious one as a result of the overcrowding in a swarm. In rubbing up against each other, change is triggered and the first thing to change is behaviour. This is a change that goes both ways, if isolated from the swarm, it can revert back to being an ordinary locust. Neurotransmitters in the brain control this, the main one being serotonin, one of the opiate-like substances that affects mood in humans.

We find human behaviour can also drastically alter in overcrowded conditions; a fact which has far-reaching ramifications in the context of design. Take the example of a school in the south of England that had particularly high levels of violence. A decision was made to surrender some classroom space in the overall design to allow for wider corridors. This was to ensure that the students less frequently 'rubbed up against each other', allowing for a more fluid passage through the building at break-times. As a result, there was a 35% reduction in violence.

We do not change in response to all input, the narrative expressed by the environment requires an influential reasoned context and meaningful associations. As I said, there are protective mechanisms in place.

We encounter many environments as we journey through our day, and there are situations we would not want to neurally mirror. Consider the medical staff I mentioned in an intensive care unit: not an environment we would want influencing our cellular make-up during the working day.

□ □

Whilst we do not change in response to all in-put, we do change if there is a context pertinent to our circumstances. That is why in a nursing home, we do not want residents viewing row upon inactive row of other elderly and infirm across a room with catheters, commodes and emergency oxygen on display... as is generally the case.

Consider the 'meaning-filled' relevant impact for the residents there, as over the weeks and months, in light of their circumstances and the personal context for them, they 'buy in' – to atrophy. They are tapping erroneous relevance, context and meaning; the system responding to an outcome that is in stark contrast to the potential revealed by the Harvard study and its bias towards vitality.

It is perhaps not so surprising that the level of depression is 3 to 4 times higher for the elderly in nursing homes than for those living with the aid of carers in the community.

7
Neurons tell a story

Historically we have tended to think of the brain as an information processor – where information goes in and comes out. Input and output. Well, the input does not just go into a file for recall. It contributes to our ever developing brain maps; these hold the patterns of our habitual ways of perceiving life and its events. We refer to these maps for interpretation as new information comes in, ever seeking associations and relevance – establishing context.

Our brain is a kind of cartographer, and as new input is evaluated against old, our maps are shaped moment to moment. It is a continually modifying process. And, even as our maps influence our interpretation of the information coming in, they are changed by that input, which then influences our ongoing interpretation. Ours is a feedback system and as information is fed back, it changes the maps that change us.

To this ongoing change we must add that the system is competitive. Professor Kandel found that as we learn new information, it causes us to increase the number of connections between nerve cells, thus reinforcing certain neural patterns. As these neural connections increase, the maps that are 'fed' prevail. If we put enough life affirming information into such a system, rather than old assumptions on atrophy, the developing maps are significantly influenced. Those geriatrics at Harvard rejuvenated within a week. The meaning embedded in the environment primed the system, and a powerful bias developed.

The installed narrative simply needs to have deeply personal context and relevance to enable prescriptive change. This is where our neural maps come into their own; via our environment they contribute to our sense of a physical feeling self. With their ever-changing records of information, our maps help us interact with our surroundings in a self 'conscious' way. In this way, our environment becomes another skin, attached to a layer of our potential. Like a baby discovering the finger he/she can see is attached to him/herself... so too our surroundings that house a reflection of our inner workings in their narrative.

I use the term 'narrative' when it comes to the meaning in a room because, like everything in life it becomes a story. A story neurologically expressed as electrical signals. I mentioned that our neurons – our brain cells – generate an electrical charge which diffuses as signals throughout our system, transforming our biochemistry. Our internal narrative is a story told as firing neurons.

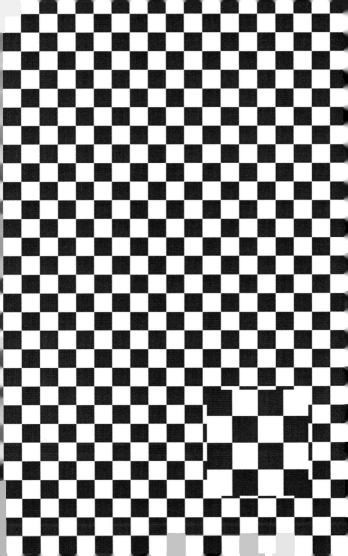

8
Primed

There was a study conducted by Benjamin Libet in 1970 where a computer was set up to give instructions to a group of participants. The technicians knew what to expect of the instructions but the participants did not – it was simply to raise ones finger. It was found that the part of the brain that registers the moving of the finger was responding in the participant's brain 400ms prior to the technician's instruction being given. Unconscious neural processing was triggered whereby the system got the message and acted on it before even being instructed; as if there was a ghost in the mechanism. It is called the readiness potential. Since Libet's experiment, in some cases there have been recordings of a readiness potential in excess of 5 seconds. A priming in the system.

I referred earlier to how our space primes us. Well, it seems we are primed at more levels than we generally consider, both consciously and unconsciously.

In our system, we have about 100 billion neurons and there are a thousand different kinds, either excitory or inhibitory.

Some of us are familiar with mirror neurons, whereby if someone smiles we automatically smile in response. Similarly we may have found ourselves yawning because someone else yawned. In fact if I wax lyrical about yawning, just reading about it here could trigger a yawn; mirror neurons mirroring that idea in the mind.

Now, if we can mirror an idea in our mind, such as a yawn, just by reading about it or seeing someone else yawn, then our mirror neurons are reflecting a certain level of priming. With mirror neurons, it seems we are priming a system primed to be primed.

Via neuroplasticity, the readiness potential, opiate triggers, mirror neurons and many more mechanisms, we are finding that the narrative embedded in the surrounding environment can prime our system to change our cells. We also find that not only is there continual change at the cellular level, whereby the narrative of the imposed surrounding design can influence the structure of the change, but biologists tell us that over a period of 7 years most of the cells in our body change. We therefore have the opportunity to influence major restructuring.

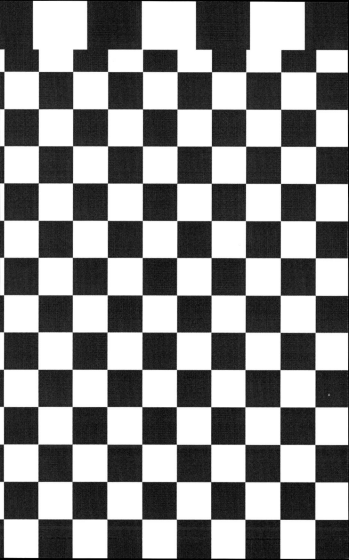

9
Real = imagined

The design of our environment has historically been perceived as an aesthetic expression and/or practical shelter, rather than something that offers metamorphosis for us the observer/occupant. Scientific endeavours in recent years and the technology to measure responses, has dramatically changed our understanding. Philosophical insights were previously the primary route for adventuresome architects, subjects such as phenomenology which for its advocates offered the essence of perception. There was parallax that offered an awareness of the subjective and objective experience of space and time as we move through a building. And the haptic realm, which focused on the sensations of touch, balance and positional awareness.

What we can now recognise is that our participation better reflects the drawing by Escher, in which the hand appears to be drawing itself. We are the neural weaver in a profound feedback loop, and are finding that as we influence change we are changing cells in the very organ that influences and interprets what we experience. A change that goes on to make further changes, that change our brain; that changes us.

Drawing hands,
by Escher

When designing the environments that surround us, becoming aware of this can help us make different choices. The more informed we are, the more consciously we can tap the creativity within our neurobiochemical design and be truly creative.

As we linger in a room with a deliberate narrative embedded there, its associations sourced from deep contextual personal references, our system changes in accordance with our interpretation of those messages. Fed by imagination and led by feelings, our neuroplastic system will continuously interpret and respond.

It is through our need for coherence woven of context, relevance and those opiate triggers, that our imagined interpretation can seem rational; enough for change to happen. Reality for each of us is based on a 'seeming logic', I say a seeming logic for it is us who determine the context and relevance that support our interpretation.

One could say we are a meaning-making mechanism.

Within this, the function of the mind appears to be – in part – to create a coherence between what we believe and the day-to-day reality of what we experience. One story seeks reinforcement from the other. In this we will find that via the doorway of our imagination, even fantasy deliberately woven into a room's narrative, with context and relevance, can prime a response to influence deliberate change. You see our imagination is capable of rationalizing fantasy as if real.

With the Harvard participants, their systems rejuvenated as the environment triggered references to their younger years as if real and in present time. An imagined experience hitched a ride.

We ever impose meaning and respond – we animate everything.

In the 1940s, psychologist Mary Ann Simmel made a simple film that involved geometric shapes – a couple of triangles and a rectangle that opened and closed at one end, as a circle moved around on a piece of paper. When the film was shown to an audience, they imagined all sorts of accompanying narratives, animating them with emotion. Some shapes were perceived to be in love, others to be stealing the circle!

Just imagine how we respond to the shapes in our environment that we endow with personal meaning… day-in-day-out.

□ □

We seed everything with meaning and respond, some people with pollen sensitivity sneeze upon seeing a plastic flower. A plastic rose lying on a tray in the bathroom may have little noticeable effect… a few neurons may fire towards a sense of it being real. Yet a plastic rose upright in a vase on a window ledge could trigger a critical shift in neural activity. Fantasy is given a context, triggering a sneeze.

We are meaning makers.

10
Over familiar

I recognise it may seem as if I am offering a life enhancing panacea here but as emphasized previously, we have to neurologically buy in, and this raises a dilemma. In a feedback system the process goes both ways; our system does not just offer vitality and rejuvenation as change, it also offers atrophy. Just as our environment can enhance our vitality it can also inhibit it, as with the example of the nursing home. It can move towards a positive outcome or a negative one, it depends on input and context.

□ □

In earlier decades, without the technology to diagnose and measure cause and effect, we had isolated evidence of a neurological response. Take the study by Professor John Bharge in the 1990s, exploring the effects of word association in some young university students. He recorded that these young participants s...l...o...w...e...d down if focusing on sentences containing geriatric associations – words like elderly or sedate. From more recent research we know that such words represented literally or through symbolic imagery in an environment cause us to slow down. Unconscious internal mind control mechanisms kick in, affecting muscle action. Ours is a responsive mind/body 'feedback' system and our neurons are continually firing in response to input. Be that towards well-being or away from it, towards or away from vitality.

Professor Kandel established that the connections between our nerve cells increase as we reinforce information. Our references to it, whatever 'it' is, become familiar. As with the maps and neuroplasticity, what Professor Kandel uncovered was that learning is competitive. With the system being mutable, ever reorganizing and renewing, as we feed our maps with the new input, we influence the maps towards the new, creating new growth.

This development of maps may seem pretty logical, yet there are all manner of paradoxes in the system. For instance, it is known that the more we remember something, the more inaccurate our memory becomes, however counter intuitive. In reinforcing new information it becomes familiar; yet, activity in the opioid rich areas is lessened as that information is repeated. So, despite the mechanism being rewarded with an opiate like rush for reinforcing the familiar, we are designed to seek the new. Then we build on that new, towards it becoming familiar, until activity in the opioid rich areas is again lessened and we seek the next new. Neuroscientists Biederman and Vessel found that ultimately mystery and the seeking of the new is preferred.

We can probably recognise that it serves our evolution to seek the new, yet resist it by holding to the familiar, until we are clear about how it serves us. The result for us when it comes to our environment and its design narrative is that as we develop a familiarity with the messaging there and at some point install the new, we then develop a familiarity with that, and change in response to it; towards the next new... and change in response to that. If we are strategic with the narrative, we can proactively participate in the how of that change.

To take this information to the level required for us to apply it to our personal room, such that the narrative we install there is influential enough to trigger the proposed change, we will need to cross reference other relevant information; thus increasing the number of connections between nerve cells in relation to it. More informed, the concept can become familiar, enough to emerge as self-evident!

As these chapters unfurl, with the information coming from diverse angles, it will stimulate multifarious pathways that compete towards integrating a new understanding.

There is not a specific page with a specific answer that makes it self evident; an understanding develops from the information scattered throughout; emerging for each of us in different ways as we each harness our own feeling-led reasoning. The initially unfamiliar and almost surreal eventually becomes… logical.

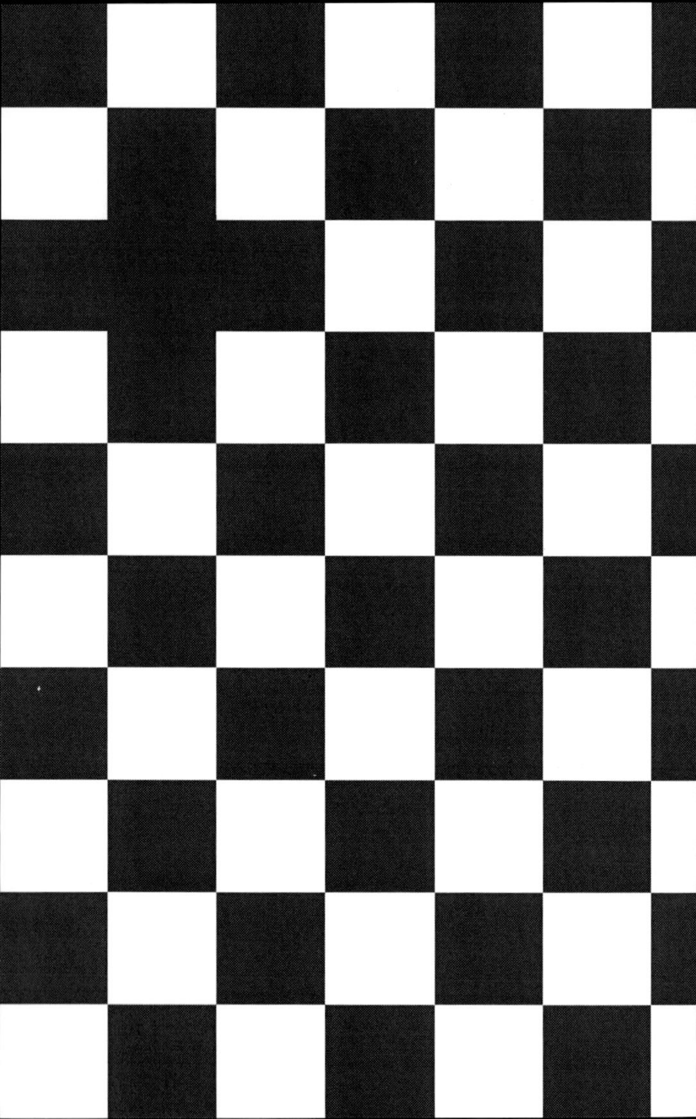

11
Foreground & background

Edward De Bono said that; *'For hundreds of years we have believed if something is logical in hindsight, then logic should have been enough to get the idea in the first place.'* Inferring this is not so, he suggests that we in fact require an informed gestation period before we 'get it' – as evidenced for us by the Harvard trial and the BBC documentary.

Some of the evidence that weaves this concept together only emerged in the last decade, some as recently as last year. Most of it was published in scientific journals and subsequently its relevance to design was not immediately apparent, though much of it related to environment.

□ □

Despite our resistance to the new, concepts can sometimes seem familiar, even if they are not generally accepted in standard practice. The fact that curves inhibit stress hormones resonates with many of us, yet surprisingly few architects use them, even in hospitals or prisons. As a concept, it has not become the norm.

If pink lowers our adrenals, one would think the odd pink wall for generic impact in a prison with violent inmates would be de rigueur. However, it is still remarkably rare for an institution to consider using it, let alone with curved walls for maximum stress-reducing effect.

In our desire to hold to the familiar some may have assumed that this information bears some relation to Eastern esoteric design ideas which have migrated West. But here we are discussing the emerging research from science on design that can change old habitual conditioning, liberate behaviours at neurological levels and even rejuvenate our cells, so quite different. I mention this because a couple of decades ago I cast my net wide and researched into the ancient Chinese art of design and the Tao. I was seeking knowledge where I could. Ultimately I stepped away from Feng Shui for reasons I will expand on shortly. But before doing so I learnt much from the Eastern philosophy and found that it fed my ongoing journey, while studying cognitive psychology and various other sciences, with reference to the environment. I learnt that the manner of our 'thinking' in the West is considerably different to that in the East. Having noted over the years that some researchers gathered information from what is present, others by what is absent, I was intrigued by the Eastern tendency to focus on background information. In the West we are more object and foreground focused, for example, if there is a scene with a bear in the foreground and mountains behind, we in the West will generally see it as a picture of a bear. The Eastern view, by contrast, will more likely be that the mountainous landscape happens to have a bear in the foreground. In other words, the Eastern focus is on the field holding the experience.

We each bring our different mindsets to the table - all of us are positioned varying degrees along a bias to fore-ground or background.

It was whilst studying different cultural perspectives that I learnt to ask different questions, the result of which deep-ened my interest in phenomenology, the haptic realm and parallax. These subjects helped me grasp emerging sci-ence differently, overall fuelling a less traditional take on cognitive psychology, which serves the ideas here well.

Despite the profound wisdom of the Tao, it was the proliferation of superstition and contradictory schools in the contemporary presentation of Feng Shui that caused me to step away. My attachment to its protocols diminished on learning that, in the 1950s, Chairman Mao had burnt all the relevant analytical charts that his people's army could find. However my respect for the Tao as a philosophy and its relevance remained.

□ □

With reference to superstition, I did acknowledge that our neural system plays with fantasy and imagination; but the latter two have a different relationship with reality due to context. The presence of a window accelerating recovery on that ward, was due in part to the neuroplasticity and those mu-opioid receptors. No need for superstitious interpretation – it was not luck.

For both Eastern and Western cultures, the boundary between real and imagined is blurred and in different ways. Context is critical, as well as taking note of new information to inform the on-going context. Though as in phenomenology and the philosophy of the Tao, we may always need the poetry.

12
Changing expectations

Our environment is not merely a shelter we respond to in a machine-like manner. We are a living organism with an embodied brain, a brain that does not just function in a linear fashion. The majority of the participants at Harvard were not rejuvenating because of wishfulness or by merely reminiscing on their younger years. Feedback fed back and their system responded at many levels. Immersed in their experience, via their interpretation in the present moment, their biological clocks were turned back. Context was critical, the doorway for such change was a coherence deep within.

Based on habit and conditioning we see what we learn to see, such that our interpretation affects us as we expect it to. If our imagination doesn't or isn't encouraged to reach towards the new, there is a tendency to reference the old; for it already has context, relevance and expectations attached. It is as if we have to reach for the new proactively, if we want change.

It is challenging to reach for the new, one of the reasons being that we tend to respond via the familiar, and that is fed by the past. There are, however, tricks for diverting ourselves towards the genuinely new, and there are ways to influence what we expect. The environment is a great facilitator for this. Its narrative can be strategically set up to trigger specific thoughts and feelings; these then lead to new ideas and those to new choices. Sometimes even changing environment due to work or family circumstances, and then incubating there in a new story, literally and metaphorically, can contribute to that.

Though we take our history with us wherever we go, we can change our associations towards it – allowing the new to develop along a less familiar path. Changing expectations.

With that in mind these chapters are not just about how to construct an environment to change feelings, they are also about learning something of how our mechanism works in relation to that change. In understanding something of how we function, we become more aware of other possibilities, offering us the chance to change our expectations. Then the new can hitch a ride.

The learning also helps build towards this information becoming self evident, and that triggers its own neural switch.

It is actually only when the information becomes self evident that we can implement the deliberate change as proposed here; that is, if we don't want the hit and miss of a placebic response. And therein lies the rub of why we may not have woven this information together before. We have only recently unveiled evidence to support the neuroplasticity, feeling led reason and opiate triggers.

Some of this information has only emerged in the last year, sufficient to make cell-rejuvenating, regenerating design credible. And, it needs to become credible for it to become familiar, so we 'get it'. I say 'get it' because we need to recognize it, to be able to apply its principles to our own surroundings... and not just pass it by.

So this is a timely dialogue, we can develop a more substantial awareness of how we function and fill in some of the blanks.

What is in our mind as real will prevail.

13
Its in the genes

And so, I come to one of our modern spiritual teachers, Ram Dass and his story in relation to aging – a story that highlights the influence of one's mind and what prevails as real.

Ram Dass was one of the adventuresome thinkers working alongside Timothy Leary back in the 1960s, experimenting with the hallucinogenic drug LSD. He became well versed in the caverns of the mind and then in his 30s he went on a different kind of mind experiment – the guru route to India. By 1997 he had become a much loved spiritual teacher with packed audiences around the globe. He spent his latter years discussing attitudes to the aging process, and therein lay a sad irony for him. Though physically and mentally vital and belying his 67 years, as he explains in his introduction in his last book – 'Still Here'; he was wondering what it would be like to be 90 years old, to have failing health and be weak limbed. He was by then an adept at meditation, having spent many years in devotional contemplation. He was familiar with letting himself go with the flow of his imagination. He took himself deep into meditation imagining himself older, weaker and infirm.

You will recall the participants in the Harvard study were influenced to focus on rejuvenation and it boosted their system; and the students in Professor Bharge's studies slowed down; but the system goes both ways, towards and away from vitality. As Ram Dass himself tells it, deep in meditation while imagining not being able to use his limbs, suddenly, he found he really couldn't use his limbs; he fell to the floor. He initially thought he was still simply in the sensorial imaginings of his meditation on being weak and infirm, only to find he really was on the floor and couldn't lift himself up. He had had a stroke. He survived but was confined to a wheelchair for the rest of his life. In light of neuroplasticity, opiate like substances and real and imagined sharing pathways, could it be that his skill at meditation and his gift for accessing sensorial imaginings caused his system to respond to his focused imaginings? Did he not so much bypass the safety protocols of the system as harness them erroneously; listening to his genuine desire to compassionately know what it was like to be infirm and debilitated?

I accept that this is not something that has been proposed about his experience – we knew so little back then. Yet it may serve to further inform the very work that had become his passion in later life – for the elderly to ignite their vitality.

What happened for Ram Dass that day we will never know, but we do now know that we can influence the neural firing and ongoing chemistry of our system.

The geriatrics in the Harvard trial reflected on vitality not frailty, and they rejuvenated within a week; 30 years later with the BBC's trial, the same. The mind in union with our brain is a powerful instrument, more than we know, and our space and its narrative can act as a guide for the focus of our neural edit.

In being strategic with how we set up our environment, we can harness a particular focus for our system to then respond to, we can steer ourselves towards preferred change. Where the boundary between real and imagined is blurred, we can even have a new narrative piggyback familiar associations, for the new to then gain access at the neural gateway. We can trick the system.

The geriatrics at Harvard rejuvenated in response to the impulses triggered by the surrounding narrative and the manipulated environment. A trick. The young students of Bharge's responded to words... and s..l..o..w..e..d down. Considering most of the cells in our body are replaced within 7 years, by influencing the neural edit, we can enhance the form of the restructuring of our mind/body.

Be strategic.

Are we grasping the potential science is unveiling when it comes to us and the impact of our environment?

I particularly ask this because of a further layer of information that is emerging in rather more evolutionary terms. I mentioned gene expression earlier. The territory of epigenetics is telling us something extraordinary that has impact on how we consider design.

Epigeneticists have recently found that patterns of inheritance may be programmed by the outer environment. The environment, which in its broader context, also includes our built environment. A few years back, scientists studying identical twins found that if they develop in separate environments, something changes in their gene expression. They cease to be identical, an experience that is handed down, affecting the inheritance of the next generation.

It seems in a man-made environment... we are mind-made.

This brings me to the arena of computer-generated design for buildings.

When it comes to design, it helps to be aware, that what the mind can conceive, it can believe and our neurology will respond. In light of this, I thought it worth mentioning that architects are today getting excited about using computer generated design to create 3D models, which are then scaled up for a real building.

Due to some of their mathematical complexities, these models have shapes that only a computer can configure. If these are shapes that only a computer can configure, in the excitement of the challenge of uncovering the engineering required to construct these as full-scale buildings, are we overlooking something?

I ask this now knowing our environments affect us more as in the metamorphosis of a caterpillar and its chrysalis, than a shell for a snail. You see, due to their complexity, these are shapes we humans cannot conceive; in us not being able to conceive them, at the level of cognition, can we believe them at the neurological level?

If not, can we really perceive and experience them in a way that serves us? Would we more likely at some level feel like visitors to these buildings, instead of part of an organic experience? Might these environments offer less meaningful experiences, or could there be some benefit for some situations, that in our still limited perspective we do not yet 'grasp'? We did not know enough to ask such questions before.

In light of epigenetics, the reference to computer-generated design, is not just about structural engineering in our buildings being adapted to suit the computer generated schemes and their benefits, or not. It is also about the neural engineering of us adapting in response to that and whether that goes on to influence our offspring. It is something we may need to consider.

When it comes to environment and evidence in fields such as epigenetics, with rejuvenation and our recovery potential revealing a dynamic connection between mind and body, we need to ask different questions. Questions that touch far more profound levels than we could imagine before we turned into this new millennium. We have to apply less familiar thinking for new times; our questions have to grow exponentially.

We are happy to debate the moral implications of genetic engineering regarding foodstuffs and stem cell engineering. Here I simply touch on architectural engineering and the implications for a susceptible system like ours and its ongoing change, the hereditary kind – it is worthy of curiosity.

If architecture is left isolated from the general sciences and their groundbreaking evidence, we may overlook some of the ramifications of new architectural ideas in the excitement of inventing them. We may also overlook emerging possibilities that could enhance our approach to design.

14
Wall to wall

We live in exciting times and the implications of what has been uncovered by the sciences in recent years is changing the game for design. It is changing our perception of what and who we are and can be. Yet, we have still been mostly ignoring the evidence, much like we did with the BBC documentary.

Our environments, where we incubate 24/7, are our chrysalis... not mere shelter. It is time for us as lay people, architects and designers to consider the emerging scientific information. For although much of its fields of study appear to be in the hands of schooled specialists, the evidence trickles down to us as our experience – so we cannot absolve ourselves of some say.

At this trickled down level, it is the arena of cognitive psychology that offers processes that we can harness to strategically design our space – once we know more.

Even gaming commerce is catching on to the benefit of understanding some cognitive psychology. For them the benefit is in understanding what happens as our minds linger in computer-generated rooms, in realities created by their games, as we sit before our screens. Our neuro-biochemical computer also plays games. In the darkened recesses of our brain, it responds to the room beyond that reflects within. It offers up a flurry of neural activity moment to moment, triggering electrochemical signals that diffuse throughout our system as a neural story.

Depending on the narrative surrounding us and our interpretation thereof, our room acts as a facilitator, in synergy with us and our two-way feedback system.

Because of how we are designed, our room, building, environment becomes a major incubator, stimulating who we become.

Many of us will have seen programmes on hoarders, their environments packed floor to ceiling, wall-to-wall – with junk… junk they 'perceive' as treasure. Broken radios found on the street, random pieces of plastic, old newspapers and clothes piled everywhere, all kinds of objects they believe they may one day repair or find a use for!! It is a behaviour considered a clinical condition. To varying degrees, there are many of us like this, with a less usual emotional attachment to our 'stuff'. The UK's institute of psychiatry says that 5% of the population are officially hoarders – that is a lot of people. It is the same statistic in the USA; that alone adds up to 15 million people having a clue to some inner neural turmoil reflected in their environment. An environment whose feedback may be reinforcing the condition.

The fashion for renting storage lockups is perhaps a less overt version of hoarding; it depends on the unnecessary excesses we are storing and the length of time we store them for. Often we store 'stuff' that holds us to the past – to old hopes and failures – more than we know.

For the 95% of us not officially considered hoarders, it is worth considering letting the excess go; for even a storage unit around the corner becomes an extension of our environment and us. We do not forget about our stuff however far away it is. Even stored around the corner it is filling an emotional gap. If it is worthy of story, we are attached, and if it was not worthy of a story we would not be keeping it. So if it is stored, consciously or not, we are attached to it.

□ □

We have places in our brain where we store all manner of references. Ever noticed, having moved the toaster, going back to where it used to be… again… and again, so ingrained is its old position in our neural theatre? Well, there is something called proprioception, this mechanism helps us to identify the location of our body in space as well as objects. When proprioceptive learning and perception weave together, they serve us well. We can attend a lecture and as the speaker refers to a place on a stage to symbolize something of his topic, that particular location referenced on the stage embraces that specific topic and its meaning for us. As he repeatedly refers to that space in his talk, we as audience hold that place spacially in our mind, such that if he then points elsewhere with reference to that topic, it can be confusing.

So, what about our 'stuff' stored around the corner, that has a place of reference in our mind? Out of sight may not be quite so out of mind as we have thought. Each of us is the best judge of whether we are hoarding, 'storing' or reminiscing.

Where a picture paints a thousand words, our environments speak volumes.

□ □

Our attachment to 'things' manifests in all manner of ways, each of us becoming attached in different ways. There is a condition that causes some people to develop an attachment to certain shapes and forms in a sexual context, including buildings. I don't mean they metaphorically find them sexy, no, they are 'literally' turned on by them. There is one woman who orgasms when she visits the Eiffel tower, another the Golden Gate Bridge, still another a picket fence.

Our surroundings and the content is meaningful, for each of us in different ways, interpretation sometimes going off the usual grid. Though what the usual grid is varies; that too is down to personal interpretation.

Perception, as I mentioned early on, is very different to seeing. As we are finding, we are a meaning making mechanism. Our interpretation of reality is ever conjured by our feeling led reasoning and opiate-firing brain… moment to moment.

15
It is how we tell it

I mentioned those experiments at the Langley Porter Institute where eye movements were correlated with neurological processes, and Wundt assessing that the muscles of the eye are connected to the muscles of the head. Over a century ago Wundt said – 'if the eye is involuntarily drawn to see something, this will trigger the head to turn towards that visual stimuli, which will in turn change the direction the entire body is moving'. This may seem logical enough but with emergent science, it puts references to parallax in a new context. If looking upwards inhibits a focus on the past and the contrary on looking down, then as we pass through a building our experience of time and space is not quite as we might generally assume. When passing through a blue room, time has even been found to 'appear' to pass more quickly than in a red room. Time is subjective, not objective as with chronological time on a clock. It is because time is subjective that we can reflect on memories.

Looking down as we move through space guides our thoughts differently, it inhibits our ability to focus on the future. In taking account of this and the neurological processes triggered by eye movements, could the influence of the environment cause one to not only think differently as one moves through the space, but also to move through it differently? And does moving through it differently further change ones thoughts and feelings?

Imagine curating an Art exhibition with this awareness, influencing the experience of the aesthetic at the heart of aesthetics. Whether the Art on display encourages us to look up and left for memory or up and right for imagination and the new, our experience will vary. What we are finding is that in union with the mechanism of perception the space surrounding us is dynamic, and at many more levels than previously understood.

It is dynamic even when we are sitting still, for we interpret based on location not just context. If we go to the theatre to watch a future based fantasy play; it will be experienced differently by the audience looking up to the stage from the Stalls than those looking down from the Royal Circle. There is also the question of whether we are stage left or right and the different neurological processes that triggers. If we are working with an ideas company and we are encouraged to look at a screen for a presentation in our conference room that is up and to the right, will our right-handed visionaries be better nurtured towards inspiration? Those advertising gurus selling their clients wares may want to consider the placement of an advert and its configuration from a whole new perspective – literally.

Gosh… who wants to keep thinking like this? Well, evidently our physiology in partnership with our neurology was designed to do so. It is what we do… day-in-day-out.

□ □

It is just that we are mostly doing it unconsciously, so, unless we are already being lead somewhere nurturing, why don't we get more consciously into the driving seat and lead it? And let's not wait another few decades before we do so. Nearly 40 years have passed since the neurological eye correlations were recorded, almost 35 years since the Harvard trial and a similar time frame since Professor Ulrich recorded that a window on a ward could help decrease a patient's required medication. The studies from the latter two illustrate the influence of mind over cellular matter as external becomes internal. The outcome for Ulrich wasn't because bright sunshine was breaking through the glass window to an otherwise sterile ward – some windows faced onto shaded light wells. Research in Japan recently found that if a view from a window on a ward is verdant – if it offers an aspect on some of nature's green – the recovery time improves even more than in Ulrich's findings.

I mentioned earlier that we feel calmer if we are surrounded by curves – electrical signals fire and an internal neurological story unfolds. If someone is given the cold shoulder – excluded from the crowd – their temperature drops. When the lights in a room are dimmed we tend to lower our voice. Ours is a meaning-making mechanism and we ever respond as we weave a story of everything.

Even random shapes offer meaning for an interpretative system like ours. I don't just mean where a symbol such as a red triangle might in one's culture tell the story 'STOP'; I mean an abstract shape apparently free of association.

Take a look at the following two shapes and the two simple made up words 'Bouba' and 'Kiki' alongside them. Make a note of which shape best reflects each word for you.

Bouba
Kiki

In tests, 98% said Bouba reflected the curved shape, and Kiki the jagged one. You possibly found the same. As we interpret, we seek associations and there is a sensorial crossover. Bouba, a made up word, triggers signals that offer meaning with reference to a softer shape. Consciously or not, we ever animate shapes and create story.

Recall Simmel's film where a couple of triangles and a rectangle opened and closed as a circle moved around a piece of paper, triggering all kinds of narratives for the audience. Some shapes were even perceived as if in love.

With feelings being primary to reason, how much more might we animate that which has personal associations for our life? Imagine the story our personal belongings tell, the meaning they exhibit. And what about the story embedded in the surrounding design?

As we live out our stories in our space, we are continually tapping and weaving emotions and reasoning, reflected in the content there as form, colour, sensations and shapes. Imbued with feeling led meaning these all act as powerful symbols of influence; telling a story we respond to whether we are conscious of it or not. It took just one week for the narrative in the Harvard trial to trigger rejuvenation for those geriatric participants. We will find we can install a deliberate story as the design for a strategic response.

For we do not just play with the surrounding narrative, as we incubate in our environment its meaning-filled content plays with us, priming us. If we neglect to impose a preferred meaning, the resident meaning will impose itself on us. Neurons fire and wire, together or apart, as trillions of cells in a sea of change of electrochemical activity move us along a continuum of change – towards or away from a certain equilibrium. Towards vitality – away from vitality. Towards atrophy – away from atrophy.

16
Hearing colour

The work of cognitive neuroscientist John Kounios and neuroscientist Irving Biederman has uncovered that the portal for inspiration is the same portal as for imagination – the anterior superior temporal gyrus. If an environment can influence inspiration, that would surely be useful to harness for science's researchers'. Creating an inspiring space for them would serve us all well. Yet in practice the opposite is often the case. Many researchers work in windowless rooms devoid of personality, packed with machines and with distracting background noise.

Today, neuroscience tells us that the design, lighting and noise on maternity wards detrimentally affects the development of newborn babies. That in itself is worthy of investigation as well as considering the side effects of such interference in our laboratories. These are environments where the researchers petri dishes for ongoing processes in their experiments are affected by the surrounding noise – and more, influencing what they are incubating. The results of which become the foundation of their research!

As researchers go from one project to another, unveiling their inspiration and seeking tenure, many cross diverse fields. Edward Vessel, one of the neuroscientists who investigated the opiate triggers along the visual pathway, went on to study our response to aesthetics in Art, and Biederman conducted research into face recognition.

With face recognition, our brain works much like a detective does with an identikit, ever seeking a match from its files. As information comes in, we build an image via association, memory and context. Facial fragments such as a nose, an eye or the turn of a brow are identified as parts of a puzzle, building towards a whole. We may recognize someone just from the curl of their lip.

When recognizing a building, we do a variation of this, looking at roof-line, window, height, orientation, texture etc. Information and associations are pulled in from different regions of the brain. In our personal room, we do much the same. With its narrative, there is form, colour, furnishings and their associations – causing stories to link up and weave with memories. The result is that clues in the form and narrative of our environment can cause other parts of a puzzle to fall into place as associations are triggered.

For those participants at Harvard, the system's ability to cross-associate via context and meaning, triggered puzzle parts that built a narrative that resonated for rejuvenation at the cellular level.

When it comes to puzzle parts, we recognize that there is no context for dark if we do not know light, or hard without a concept of soft. Neuroscientist Professor Antonio Damasio proposed that in 'knowing soft', we are also sensing the quality of its 'softness'.

Take the chairs we are sitting on. They are not only hard or soft beneath us as a design feature: if hard we are aware of the hardness, if soft, the softness. This affects our neural signals, it is subtle but we respond. This subtle response integrates other sensations, to the degree that our chair can affect our overall mood; a mood that can affect our wellbeing. The quality of its softness can even trigger memories.

At the office the touch of a hard chilled glass table beneath the document we are signing, affects us differently to the warmth of a walnut one. Then there is the detail of whether it is a curved desk or a rectangular one and the differing experiences of that.

The design of our office is more than surface deep. What are we creating, as interpretation does its thing and visceral sensations invade our thoughts, even as opiate-like substances are triggered and affect our experience at work? Some people say the job is killing them, could design change this?

Sensations received through our senses and filtered via perception contribute to our stories. Neurons fire and signals diffuse throughout our body, the locus of our experience. The softness of a chair stimulates a response, as does the size and shape of it and the rest of the furnishings. This even extends to the location of the room in relation to colleagues we feel supported by – or not. I know we don't want to think like this but we do anyway, consciously or not. We are a feedback meaning making system. All our experiences affect us at the neurological level, influencing our interpretation as senses cross over. All the way from the minutiae to... epigenetics.

Think of the alchemy involved for a neural story to trigger recovery for those patients on the ward as they lay in bed, the window playing its part, day-in-day-out. Moment-to-moment. Senses continually cross over where not only can a shape become a sound but a sound can become a shape; be that the sound of 'Bouba' or the cushioned seat beneath us, triggering all manner of responses.

With Kiki and Bouba we are not just reading the words, we are hearing them too. Expressions like 'a soft sound' or 'a loud colour' make sense because our senses cross over. Some people with a condition called synesthesia see colours when they look at numbers, others hear colour.

Professor Antonio Damasio found that we can even respond to imagined sounds as if real. With the real and the imagined sharing pathways at levels far beyond our previous ken, he found that patterns in the auditory cortex correspond to what subjects heard in their 'mind's 'ear'. Not a sound they physically heard, but a sound they allowed themselves to 'imagine'. Feelings, sounds, thoughts and more, criss-crossing over as imagination weaves with interpretation and signals fire.

So , where does this take us with design?

Well, as neurons fire and all manner of sensations are triggered, the electrochemical signals within the body merge as a story in the mind. Senses cross over and as they do, so do the thoughts and associations that frame our experience. The story in our mind crosses over as neural signals.

Now, when it comes to these stories in the mind, metaphors are a great facilitator to frame a relevant design – they cross over too. They tell one story in terms of another. In the metaphor,' free as a bird', there is a cross over from 'free' – to – 'a bird'.

Metaphors paint pictures in the mind. Say 'free as a bird', and try not to see a bird... did you see one? They offer up pictures to which we attribute meaning, pictures that offer different meaning for each of us. Such pictures, when used to frame a design, transform a room into an incubator for that story. They can embed the narrative with deep meaning; allowing the design to frame complex feelings, circumstances and concepts.

Long considered the language of the imagination, metaphors have been found to emerge at the aforementioned anterior superior temporal gyrus. One can assume that there is a reason for them to share this particular doorway with imagination and inspiration.

Metaphors can be distilled to a shape, colour or sensation, and in telling one story in terms of another, that colour or shape can tell the story. Neuroscientists now know we can place just the shape of an idea before us, like a metaphor, and our system will build a structure around it. With metaphors, their representation penetrates our psyche through contemplation as we incubate in their narrative. Used in the design they can tell a strategic story, a story we may only have pictures, shapes and colours in our mind for, that are attached to sensations, imaginings and inspiration. In this way metaphors can give us access to the neural gateway and a choice for a story in our room we may not have words for, but that can touch our representation of freedom or success – or whatever our choice.

If our personal metaphor for freedom happened to be – 'free as a bird' – we could examine how this might inform a design. If 'free as a bird' had a colour – what would it be? What shape and texture would it have? The answer for each of us would, of course, be different. Asking that simple question might inspire us to make a more creative choice, though the cognitive process for the profound change proposed in this book is more complex than this. The above example is simply to illustrate that metaphors come in all shapes and sizes, and can tap our personal representational system and frame a design with a goal, one we may not have specific words for.

Image and interpretation are each powerful themselves, the union of both as in a metaphor seeding and framing a design, can be profound.

Metaphors can touch the depth and breadth of emotions and sensations we don't always have specific words for. This is how an otherwise intangible story can be told in an environment via just a colour. As a frame for the narrative of a design, metaphors are able to take us where we would go if we had access to our inspiration and passions. They can give us access at the neural gateway, where even the new can hitch a ride. Used in context, as one story is told in terms of another, they can prime our system with inspiration or freedom – whatever emerges for us, and do so via the design. They work in synergy with our story telling, meaning-making system. So this is not something clever as regards design, merely a logical approach... once one understands more about how the system works.

☐ ☐

Our system is story based, as cognitive neurolinguists George Lakoff and Mark Johnson said in The Philosophy of the Flesh, 'The human conceptual system is metaphorically structured and defined'.

When personal and relevant, metaphors can be used as powerful game changers for design. They touch far more than the individual words that compose them, thanks mostly to the meaningful pictures they paint that emerge from our personal imagination… and all that they can touch. They connect to our personal story and its puzzle parts via our ever switched-on interpretative mind.

As the visionary thinker of the 1950s Gregory Bateson said of metaphor; 'That is how the whole fabric of mental interconnections holds together. Metaphor is right at the heart of being alive.'

□ □

With respect to Neutra, it is time to weave this under-standing and some cognitive awareness into a new approach to architecture and design, and uncover how our room might serve us better. Help it tell our new story, that we may live it.

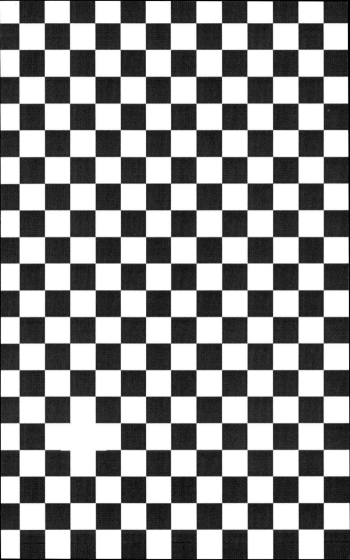

17
Hitching a ride

As we turned into this millennium science was on an exciting threshold. With new technology measuring the previously immeasurable, earlier areas of research that had been side-lined could be revisited with a different spin. As Biederman and Vessel found, when re-examining the old evidence on mu-opioid receptors increasing in density along the visual pathway. Today, the neurological sciences are sharing a deeper dialogue with many fields – we have neuropsychology, neurolinguistics, neurophysiology, neurobiology, neurophysics and many more.

With easier access to these territories, and having learnt something of metaphor when I studied cognitive neurolinguistics,I began looking at how our personal narrative emerges and how susceptible we are to its bias. I wanted to learn about the impact of language as a tool to express thoughts and feelings, with the intent of finding a way to use the language of metaphor and its pictures to strategically frame a 'persuasive' design. It needed to be a design where the narrative could impact us at a deep-seeded level.

With this in mind I also studied hypnosis. I wanted to gain a better understanding of our susceptibility to suggestion. I hoped to uncover a way for our room to become an incubator, where a strategic design could frame our preferred story to influence change.

Just as metaphors can be distilled to a shape, colour or sensations to represent a story in our mind, that story when manifested contributes to creating an hypnotic experience. One that can have impact on us 'day-in-day-out' at a deep representational level.

When it comes to the story in a room capturing our focus, neurologist V.S.Ramachandran proposes; *'there may be much going on simultaneously as we enter a room but as we funnel our focus, some elements draw more attention than others'*.

Just as the emphasis of parts of a story in the design of a room's narrative can draw our focus , how we tell parts of the story in our mind also affects us. The emphasis on certain words affecting the meaning, as illustrated with the following sentence. As it repeats, read each line emphasising the different emboldened words. Note how each time you change the word, its emphasis subtly changes the meaning of the overall sentence.

I did not say I loved design.
I **did** not say I loved design.
I did **not** say I loved design.
I did not **say** I loved design.
I did not say **I** loved design.
I did not say I **loved** design.
I did not say I loved **design**.

With the following sentence, note how, as you read the end part, the mind fills in the gaps... 'whrbeey we can siltl make snese of it and its mneanig eevn thugoh it is selpt wnorg'.

When we enter a room, not only can we be influenced by the focus, but we unconsciously fill in the gaps between the focal points and the embedded meaning. A subtle shift in emphasis in the design can offer a different experience, dependent on how the narrative is interpreted within our mind, via its context and relevance. The same room can tell a different story for different people, for the story unfolds inside our mind with reference to our own associations and focus. Different from phenomenology where sensations and images exist via the meaning they exhibit to the observer, here we are finding even the language we use opens and closes neural doors.

Recall that Professor Bharge's participants slowed down just by contemplating slowness as they wrote words associated with being elderly. Imagine the influence of the language of our imagination where metaphors – like that bird flying free – harness colour, form and more, to tell a deep relevant story.

Instead of it just being a metaphor as a story, it is a story told in terms of a design and its representational details of colour, sensations, images etc. So, a feeling is told as a metaphor, that is then used to frame a design, whereby the room itself becomes a metaphor that we immerse ourselves in.

18
Tricky tricky

Hopefully you will have realized that this is not simply about sourcing a feel-good metaphor and seeding its details of form, colour and more into the design. That alone won't do the trick – not for the kind of impact we are discussing. Learning about how the system works helps us source our relevant, contextual and meaning filled metaphors at a more relevant, meaningful contextual level. A powerful metaphor can emerge, one that allows us to tap deep into our potential via its associations in our environment. Broader knowledge helps us make more informed choices that have a greater personal resonance. Offering the seed for a truly nurturing design, one that touches the brilliance at our core – and all that can offer.

The degree to which we can influence the impact our environment imposes is phenomenal... and reflects a certain trickiness within our system.

Every day of our life we trick ourselves; sometimes erroneously and often unconsciously. Why else would anorexics buy into being fat, some killing themselves as a result of starving their system? For them something they imagined hitched a ride – erroneously. Those rejuvenating geriatrics tricked themselves too but – positively. What we are finding is that where real and imagined share pathways, we can strategically trick our tricky system and allow the calculatingly preferred, even the new, to hitch a ride. Ultimately, the trick is not something that goes on out there, it goes on in here, in our brain.

Whilst studying hypnosis, I learnt that no-one hypnotises us. Rather we allow the hypnosis to take place – we facilitate it. Our neural system was designed with many safety protocols. With hypnosis, our willingness to open to the suggestion of the hypnotist is measured by the degree to which we allow them to allow us to influence ourselves; basically, we enable the process.

Those who say with conviction that something isn't possible are hypnotizing themselves – we just haven't labelled it self-hypnosis. There are of course extenuating circumstances, be that physiological, familial,cultural, political and so on. But generally in life, when things go wrong, it is more often than not because we genuinely bought into that which was erroneous. When they go right,we also bought in, but into that which was nurturing.Pessimists often point to the negative outcome in a situation to illustrate that they were right to not be optimistic; but perhaps expectations fed the outcome. As Henry Ford said; 'Whether you think you can or you think you can't – you're right'.

We continually trick ourselves, as image and context cross the divide between the physical and the psychological. That window on the ward enhanced recovery and the verdant view more so, neural tricks via the imagination.

Anyone who thinks they have no imagination – think again – feel again; we are pure imagination. A self-organizing, self-renewing, opiate influenced neural system, where our experience and emergence is an act of creation.

All of us have that part of the brain that fires up the imagination – the anterior superior temporal gyrus – the same region that fires up for inspiration and metaphor.

In a system where it seems life is a story, we find they are stories that we can make up; where the unfolding chapters are built on illusions and held in place by their relationship with other illusions and their stories. The wonder of it all is the degree to which we can influence the unfolding plot via the 3D theatre of our animated room. Our room acting as an incubator, influencing whom we choose to become; a choice we can change any time we choose.

For every day we create a synopsis Hollywood would be proud of... there is always story.

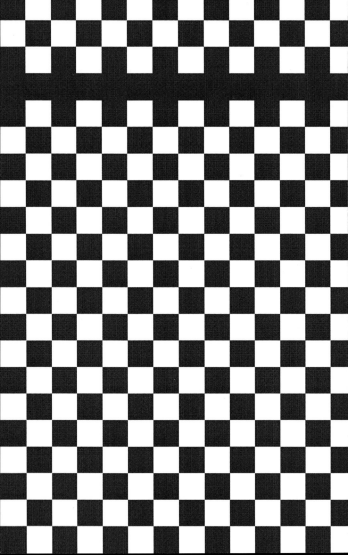

19
Vibrational illusions

When making a decision, or attempting to come up with a new idea, many of us have experienced a mental block. 'We give up, head off for a coffee break... and suddenly, inspiration hits'. Our right brain connects disparate information and a resolution to a prevailing problem emerges. Though left and right brain share information and are both involved in the processing, it is the right hemisphere that offers up that 'A-haa' moment.

☐ ☐

Daily, we deal with a vast input of information that requires massive editing, our right brain firing off as our system filters and interprets the relevant from out of a vast context.

That is part of what happens when metaphors tell one story in terms of another, they have the ability to reduce to the relevant. Einstein harnessed a visual metaphor when imagining what it would be like to travel on a beam of light, and it offered up inspiration via the anterior superior temporal gyrus for the formula $E=MC^2$. Though that picture in his mind painted a thousand words, its resolution out of a multitude of possibilities was edited to one emergent choice out of the many. With Einstein's formula in which E = energy and MC^2 = mass at the speed of light in a vacuum, it is one story told in terms of another. $E=MC^2$ is a metaphor. The story of mass told as energy, where mass and energy are interchangeable.

I touch on particle physics here, for where nothing is what it seems neurally, it turns out nothing is what it seems materially. Tables and chairs dissolve beyond the atomic 'touch me-feel me' experience to particles of vibration.

Einstein, Heisenberg, Bohr and many other eminent physicists proposed in the early part of last century that everything in our world exists as dynamic oscillating energy. Vibration. As physicists tell it, the component parts of vibration are particles. With each particle, 0.0001% is apparently physical, the other 99.9999% is spinning nothingness. Yet, were we to examine the 0.0001% that is apparently physical we would find that 99.9999% of that is also spinning nothingness. And the 0.00001% of that which appears as a physical impulse is again 99.9999% spinning nothingness. And within that and within that... and on... and on. An analogy would be unravelling our material world as one would a vibrational virtual Russian doll... towards nothingness. Illusionary material reality, not even dust. Yet from this nothingness emerges our atomic experience as a vibrational somethingness that we can touch and feel. It is the components of this that we call design. Our workplace, home, its walls, tables and floors are all vibrating particles of life's force, separated by frequency.

Where the real and the imagined share neural pathways and illusions can emerge as our perceived reality, I found it rather appropriate that spinning atomic 'touch me – feel me' somethingness emerges from spinning particles of nothingness.

At the particle level, physicists tell us that we only get to see and feel a wall as solid in our 'touch me – feel me' world because our human measuring device – the body – is just about adequate to allow us to do so. They tell us that we may feel separate to our environment and its components parts may seem separate to us, but we, and our surrounding space are part of a continuous field of interactive vibrating particles, separated by frequency. Within the billions of particles that constitute the bulk we experience as a solid mass, an extraordinary subatomic vibrational world is at work.

In 2008, the same year he received the Isaac Newton Medal, eminent physicist Anton Zellinger and his team in Vienna unveiled evidence supporting a surreal idea that was first proposed decades before by the fathers' of quantum physics. The possibility that 'unless there is a conscious observer reality does not exist as we know it'. You may want to read that last sentence again!

Observation in the particle world is not passive, nor is it in our neurological world. We contribute to what we see. If we look at the image of the Necker cube below, we will see the rectangle in the forefront suddenly flips. Whichever is forefront for you on the cube, 'a or b'... wait for the other to 'flip' to the forefront.

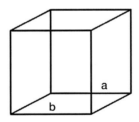

The Necker cube

This flip with the necker cube is only partly voluntary – it moves in our mind not in physical reality. Observation is not passive and even has an interdependence with our ability to think.

With eyes closed, and using your mind's eye, imagine the corner of your room down by the skirting. If you prefer, do this with eyes open by watching a real corner in your room, down by the skirting. Keep looking as if waiting for a mouse to come around the corner, except you are actually watching that corner for your next thought to appear. Try it, watch and wait for your next thought. You will find that no thoughts arise – when you are looking for them none appear. Observation can inhibit the thought process. Observation and perception are far more active in our experience of our reality than we have known.

20
Imagination

Biederman and Kounios found that inspiration often arises when one is caught in the illusions of day-dreaming, it is then that thoughts and ideas spring to mind.

Imagination.

All of us are designed to imagine, each of us emerging with our own spin on what we call real.

Most of us don't think of our imagination as real. Apart from anything else, part of its role is to invent. So imagination is about that which is not here, yet it contributes to what we 'imagine' is real. In the sciences some look to the seat of consciousness to discern what might be real. One of the definitions of consciousness is our ability to have an experience and know we are having one, resulting in what we think of as real. Whatever may unfold about the role of imagination in this, by recognizing that nothing is what it seems, we can at the least use our imagination to help us find a way to feel good.

Scientists have found that the prefrontal cortex is triggered when we feel good. This is a region of the brain that also controls 'attention' – our ability to be selective in our focus. If the environment is set up to help us feel good and the prefrontal cortex is triggered when we feel good – then while there we continue to feel even better. We are enhancing our 'attention' and if that attention is on the narrative of the design surrounding us – that already makes us feel good – then that feel-good experience is intensified. Get the life enhancing potential built into the system.

To take this feel-good factor to the world of bricks and mortar and the story told by our personal space, we find that a new aspirational story has been emerging in the marketplace over the last couple of decades. It is brand weaving with lifestyle as the new feelgood and it has infiltrated architecture... our chrysalis.

This was noticeable a couple of decades ago when fashion designers were turning ghetto cool into a marketing art form. For architecture the genre of graffiti art emerging downtown was reflected in artist style lofts emerging as boho chic uptown. A decade later with the aid of the internet, the fashion for architecture as a branded image went viral. In the years since, apartment blocks have risen up all around the globe – in London, Manhattan, Brazil, Melbourne, Tokyo – emphasizing the trend for a tailored club cut for a new youth culture. A style where musac plays at party volume in the lobbies and mood-lit corridors act as catwalks for the guests to strut their stuff. Commercially minded building developers have been rolling out carbon-copy concepts, much as one would copy a designer label.

The thing is… the brand experience of architecture is different to that of products such as clothes that we wear or gadgets that we use. We fully immerse ourselves in our environments. With their story, they act as a chrysalis towards change. A jacket does not.

If we buy a jacket we can wear it differently from some-one else. We are all a different size, shape and colour, we can team it with different garments and change acces-sories through the seasons. But with architecture, fur-nished with a branded concept, a collective of residents are living in the same architectural outfits everyday. I was wondering how an interior story, shared by a crowd yet separated behind their front doors... might affect the chrysalis experience.

The difference between today's developments and the row upon row of terraced housing in the 1950s or the cul-de-sacs of the 60s, is that we have become a culture attached to life-style and brand like never before. The reach of our aspirations has changed.

So it would help to recognize when it comes to environ-ment, that there may be ramifications if we don't allow our incubator – our space – to reflect our personal inspira-tion, as opposed to a collective aspiration.

In my design company, though I originally developed one-offs, at the end of the 1990s I was involved in the birth of a major apartment concept. Though it appeared to be about individuality, it actually told a lifestyle story in a less than individual way; it was harnessing crowd membership to its own lifestyle. It was 'one size fits all' masquerading as differentiation. A collective were sharing in an aspirational story. I was curious about the social and cultural impact.

In these earlier years, we were less aware of epigenetics, neuroplasticity, neural triggers and internal opiate rewards. We weren't reckoning on the neural impact of brand as it exploded off the pavement into the environment, and from there imploded inside our brain.

As I unveiled the science, I realised that I was witnessing something much more profound than an evolution of style. I began to wonder how an homogenised setting might affect our experience and what then happens to our 'free flying bird'. I was also considering whether we could harness this susceptibility of ours and the phenomena of brand and lifestyle in our environment to our advantage.

If there is the possibility of losing something with computer-generated upscaled 3D models, I was wondering if we could gain something with lifestyle. Could we create life-enhancing concepts with the cumulative effect of such a collective? After all, critical mass creates critical change. Where brand is often regarded as superficial, it could then be used to nurture and add a meaningful story to a space.

Many architects involved in the master planning of cities are aware of social issues and the impact of the environment, but less so of the contemporary evidence emerging from research in genetics, neuroscience et al.

Here we are learning that, immersed in our immediate surroundings, not only do we change over time, but epigenetics has revealed that such change is also influenced by the place where we grew up. So not just the effect of a room or a building, but the larger environment.

There is the expression common to city dwellers, 'you can take the girl out of – [as in my case] – Liverpool, but you can't take Liverpool out of the girl'. Or New York, Tokyo, Sydney and on across the globe. More than just culturally, it seems it is neurally so, all the way down to our gene expression. This is where we find that lifestyle is connected – in part – to our gene expression.

So for those who buy into lifestyle it is not just about a fashion moment – at a profound level it is more than that. Influenced by our herding instincts, brand and lifestyle tap and prime our need to belong. Touching our drive to develop and evolve.

To propose that lifestyle is somehow calculated into the evolutionary plan can sound outrageous... except... epigentics is revealing a core priming mechanism in our evolutionary path. Though I should mention it is not about owning something by Louis Vuitton or wearing cool trainers. It is more about the drive that gets us wanting to own them and the story inherent to that.

We are meaning-makers and all our stories inform us even as they shape who we become. So how about if, in light of this, we shake design up a bit? We are already understanding that time is subjective. Back in the 1950s, 40 was the new 50 – people appearing older than their years, and today we declare that 50 is the new 40 – younger than our years. It is worth asking if this is a reflection of some priming from our youth-biased lifestyle?

Since we all have a suggestible neuroplastic system, and all our stories are subjective, more informed, we have the ability to be proactive with the influence we set up. So... what if we took some of the youth bias in branding to nursing homes? Take a life-enhancing attitude to the drawing board there, and treat these as places to live with vitality, rather than to house assumed atrophy. Let us not assume these to be places to retire or die. Not now that we know about our neuroplasticity, epigenetics, opiate-like triggers and the impact of beauty... to name a few.

When it comes to being elderly and atrophy, our mechanism isn't ageist – we are. Or I should say our conditioning is. Harvard simply flashed a beam of light onto other possibilities that are less familiar.

How about geriatrics living in the loft concepts usually associated with a younger generation, with musac playing in their lobbies? Perhaps the youth culture which might normally choose to live in studio loft spaces could live as a collective in a hotel-like facility, with shared sitting and games rooms. A young version of a retirement home, but with a whole other assumed attitude. Give them opportunities for a more varied social life than that which current workmates or old friends offer. Mix it all up a bit for the opportunity for change. After all, the only difference for the geriatrics at Harvard and those in the nursing home was where their perception took their mind.

So this is not only about rejuvenation and liberating our passions via the design for a new tomorrow today – it is also about our vitality, that we usually associate with youth. We all buy into story, old and young, so let us set up a story seeded in the metaphor that frames the design surrounding us, that harnesses our vitality. Whatever our age, we all have cells that ever renew and reorganize.

Then our proverbial view on youth being 'wasted on the young' – may be re-visited.

Where lifestyle may have been perceived as superficial, it can tap something quite profound. However , if we aren't 'mindful' we could pass it by, as we did with the BBC programme.

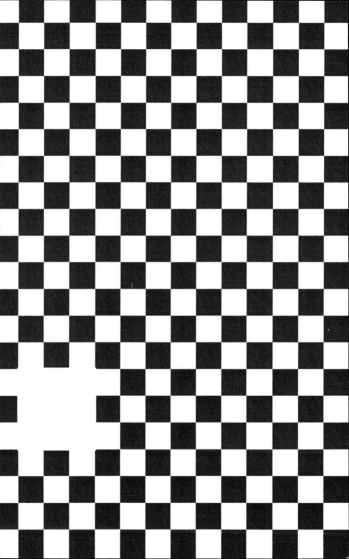

21
Interpretation

However trivial design may have previously appeared, as a pattern within our genius mechanism it can affect us all the way down to the core of who and what we are – and what we can become. Design is deeper than we have assumed. It is not just about iconography, it can inform and shape us even as we shape it.

The cubism of the Art world illustrates how easily we identify meaning with very little line and apparent content. What might happen when our 3D room is filled with personal meaning? Recall the Necker cube and how its image flipped. What happens when that cube is our room with all the multidimensional sensations, interpretation, context and relevance flipping there. Perception is not passive, our imagination and associations contribute to what we see.

I mentioned the process of proprioception earlier. We know this isn't just about holding focus in a lecture theatre. Even when we look at our favourite ornament, part of our system prepares information for the movement that would be required 'if' we were to pick it up, we become aware of its shape, size and location. If we were to hold it or move it in our hand, the ornament moves in a space inside our brain. There would also be all the associations of who gave it, when and why. All of this information going on as we link feelings, associations and motor reflexes.

Beyond all the influential 'stuff', there is also the effect in an environment of looking up and down, right or left and the neurological processes that triggers. Then there are the personal objects, photos and references to our circumstances, family and colleagues that we continually note. Be that office or home. We think, feel and observe in our space. We reflect, anticipate, work, sleep, eat and commune there. If it is home, it is the place we love and share in relationships and have our fears and dreams unfold. We can be private with ourselves there, even as the technology of the internet, TV and radio brings the world to us. We even inherit the geometry and meaning of its location, be that Vienna, Tokyo or Liverpool.

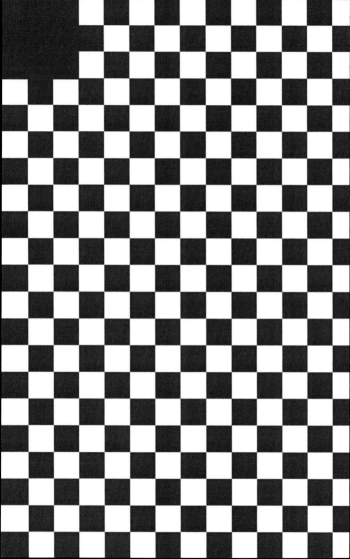

There is so much going on every micro-moment. If the stillness of Zen is the effect we are planning in a generic sense, we may wish to consider how to achieve 'nothing' – 'no thing'. Our system is always busy – it is about the focus we set up and our interpretation while there.

If we are willing to uncover our metaphor for stillness at a deep 'unconditioned' level and embed that in the design – then we are really harnessing the potential of our system and its faculty of focus and all that can facilitate. Whether our story of choice is stillness, vitality, aspiration or rejuvenation, sourced via our personal metaphor and embedded in the design, it will trigger our representational system.

If we weave a narrative into our environment that touches the heart of our psyche, as Neutra wished, our hypnotic space becomes our accessible friend. By sourcing our liberating metaphors and allowing their form to frame the design, our environment becomes our incubator towards nurturing change. Whatever the choice of surface elements – be that hard edged steel, concrete, soft velvet padding, cool sheet glass or the carved mastery of oak – whatever emerges as our choice for the materials, each will project a different vibe, and differently for each of us. Hard edge steel may well soften one person's spirit and bruise another's.

Perhaps the city broker with a razor sharp minimal apartment in town would prefer to immerse in birdsong and a beach to inspire excellence. That may be a beachside retreat, literally or metaphorically, via some décor that nurtures that beach in the mind.

If that space happens to be on the 40th floor and has a French faux juliette balcony to offer a sense of escape in the mind, the balcony can allow a sense of liberation in the imagination; an aesthetic escape rather than physical – while still safe at altitude. Though whether it offers a freeing sense or an isolating one depends on the room's story - the one we are incubating in; and where it takes ones mind.

Ultimately it is down to interpretation and context. Walls do not a prison make... we do.

□ □

There is always our story... it is just about how we choose to tell and interpret it. We can be strategic and tap the story that contributes to a life more fully lived.

The psychological and the physical are continually crossing boundaries, as the story 'out there' reflects inside our mind. Inside our mind where, if we look at velvet,there is a sensorial crossover and we can virtually feel it. We can recall a sad moment and sense it, then spin our emotions 180° just by reflecting on a joyous time in our life; immersing ourselves in all the chemical rushes that that engenders.

As with Simmel's film, we attach story to form. We can visualise a blue square with our eyes closed, and then change its form so that it becomes a red circle. Psychologists have found that if we elicit a specific emotion or deep symbolic reference for that blue square – in then consciously changing its shape and colour, we change something of the emotional charge attached to it, and its deep seeded narrative.

Our internal neural language is pattern recognition, when we mentally change that shape a different pattern and its story emerges within.

When we play with interpretation we are playing with our chemistry. By changing the 'symbolic' shapes, colour and sensations of the story within our space we access our representational system, and change our internal neural story.

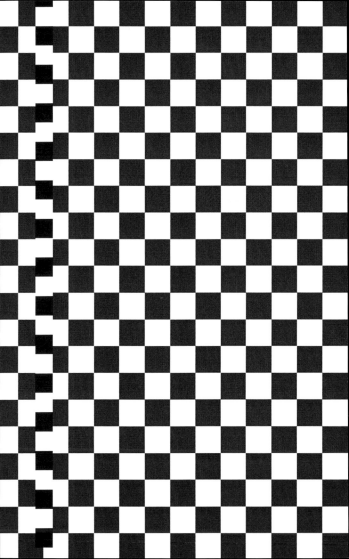

22
Up close and personal

As regards that internal story, beyond the herding tendency and brand temptation we have touched on, when it comes to design, our physical fingerprint hints at something of our individuality having a major part to play in all of this.

Each of us is cut from a fabric with at least 7.5 billion pattern differentials, differentials illustrated on that tiny patch of flesh at the tip of our finger. A patch woven from differing synaptic structures as neurons self-organized at birth, to produce our particular fingerprint.

It is a differential that may offer a clue for us to reach beyond our conditioning, to our individual. It's position at the tip of our finger certainly allows our fingerprint to act as a visible reminder of our individuality, one more visceral than tying a knot in a handkerchief.

Whether it mainly acts as a security identity print or not, our fingerprint would appear to hint at something more valuable even than rejuvenation and vitality via design, or our personal sense of beauty with its immune boost and tolerance. For it reminds us of that most elusive of qualities – though it be our birthright – our personal authenticity that underpins our one in 7.5 billion. The 'I' in me; as individual as our personal metaphor.

We have all met people we clicked with, even looked like; who thought like us, responded like us, shared similar traits and interests – yet we still had a different fingerprint. The visible 'I'.

Many of us at some point, have found ourselves questioning with that 'I' – what do 'I' really want and who am 'I'? Some when young, others when older. Imagine identifying what that may be, and via our personal metaphor, being able to create an environment that actually supported its emergence as we incubated in its related narrative.

Whatever the generic design and influences going on around us, imagine if our environment could reinforce that profound sense of the personal; that might be somewhere high on a wish-list. An environment offering us a chance to create a narrative through design that tempts us to liberate ourselves to a deeper sense of self. Our alchemy set free from conditioned framing.

Whatever our faith or philosophical inclination, I doubt it will be superficial stuff that will concern our particular self when our time comes to exit this world: it will more likely be about how well we lived and perhaps our legacy. In that, it may matter that we lived who we are, expressed our personal pattern. If we build on that, free of some of the social, cultural and familial conditioning we have acquired, then not only may we feel more content and inspired, but those paths that speak of the god or self within, may better resonate.

We would be taking a lead from Emerson: 'Do not go where the path may lead – go instead where there is no path and leave a trail.

Our own.

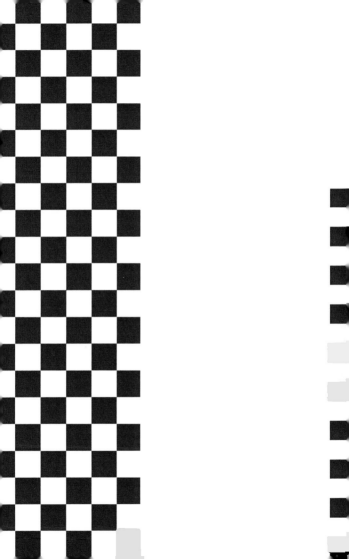

23
Origins

The rules we thought we functioned within are manoeuvring before our eyes. Literally 'before our eyes'. Our visual pathway and those mu-opioid receptors have a major part to play. Via perception woven with imagination the influence of our environment goes all the way to our core generative cells. Even to our evolution, for we are designed to respond to our environment and its inherent meaning. Be that our room, building, town, city... and on, influencing our gene pool to the degree that not only can I not take Liverpool out of the girl, but I can't take Vienna out of her either. It seems Vienna was not just an influence for Neutra, but for me too – via my father and the generations before him. Science has unveiled evidence that the place where our parents grew up affects ongoing generations.

Our surroundings and those of our ancestors influence us at levels we could not have imagined a decade ago. The Italian immigrant from the fishing coast of Sicily whose children now live in Harlem, the Ethiopians coming from vast desert plateaus whose children today play in a Welsh village – their genes still touched with the potential to express those ancestral deserts and oceans.

It is time to awaken to a new conversation in design.

□ □

When it comes to our day to day choices in design, lifestyle magazines bombard us with images of current trends and the lives of our heroes and heroines, and how they find succour. We are seduced to join the party, we want to belong so we reach for the herd. But our lives can become typecast 'aspirational' rather than 'inspirational aspirational', unless we stay alert to the whisper from within. Our personal metaphors can tap that whisper and nurture us if they frame the design. Restoring us.

Though to others, our space may seem like a place that just looks and feels good – to us it will be a place from which we project our talent, health, inspiration, our success, ourselves, into the world. However we dress it, as trad, eclectic, modern or undress it in zen, whatever is our style of 'choice', it becomes our nurturing chrysalis.

Which colour do you think is more likely to trigger inspiration, a pastel green that looks delightful on a paint chart, or the story inherent to the wonderful tone of the corn blue dawn sky outside our window in the Dordoigne from last spring when we celebrated winning a dream project? Or perhaps it is a colour that comes to mind when pondering on an unbounded dream, or a blue that changes our sense of time.

One might consider that painting the walls the colour of that dawn sky in the Dordoigne, with its positive associations, is the one to go for to trigger a nurturing response… while playing safe in a 'feeling good' kind of way! This is how some people make their choices, if taking the trouble to be reflective and wishing to create a more meaning-filled environment. They remember what felt good, where and when, and then recreate that. Here though, we are aware of the system's larger maps and based on those, that corn blue of 'the Dordoigne' won't necessarily nurture the new. It may trigger the memory of a successful time but it is an old one and therefore tied across old neural firings and their maps. So, though it triggers positive memories, it could be limiting as it touches parts of other less nurturing stories that were earlier embedded.

Think on Anna who, having ambitions for her son Frank to be an architect, had gone what I call – the Dordoigne route – in other words – her reasoned route. She had placed froebel geometric blocks and pictures of buildings in his bedroom during his younger years. Anna wanted to influence her son's imagination, as she saw it, in a positively nurturing way – towards being an architect.

As he matured, Frank responded to the hypnotic environment and the aspirational images strategically placed there by his mother. Note aspirational not inspirational. Frank Lloyd Wright went on to become one of the finest architects of his time. Though the strategic design imposed by his mother contributed to achieving her goal, to be provocative, however talented Wright was as an architect; perhaps given more personal freedom for his own inspiration as a child, he may have chosen differently as an adult. Or perhaps simply more freely the same. He may have benefited from the limitless horizons that a freer inspired choice engenders, one that touched his personal passions for his free bird – his genius obviously had reach.

As for that delightful pastel green, its influence pales in light of what we can harness. And the colour that came to mind on pondering an unbounded dream, that could be the one to offer a portal towards change and the new; for beyond its presenting fantasy may reside deep untapped passions. We can harness those to strategically inform the design choices, be that via curves or angles, hard or soft surfaces, whatever details of form emerge to represent the story at a deep meaningful level. Along with the influence of the colour, incubating in those details as a system that renews and reorganises in response to a story that has context and relevance, we can spread our wings.

And get ready to be as free as a ....

Victor Frankl, the eminent neuroscientist, suggests in his philosophy of mind that life has no meaning save the one we give it. In honour of his insight… and of emerging science… along with a nod to Neutra, I suggest that we let our room mean something – that our life may mean more.

24
What now?

The subtle questions and answers that lead to our metaphors and their design components, need to be executed in a sequential manner. In a two dimensional book format such as this, that is not possible. Apart from anything else, if the process was written here, there is the tendency for some of us to look ahead to check it out; thus disturbing the sequence and undoing the spontaneity required to reach that which is new and less conscious. To stir the passions, the process requires the sequencing, inspiration, spontaneity, moments of daydreaming and a setting that triggers the senses and less familiar imaginings. Some may want pictures to stimulate ideas, others sounds and scents. I have composed a detailed process that takes us into all manner of fantasy, loosening old framing, teasing the imagination towards change and our inspiration in a relevant, contextual way that focuses on design in relation to the personal … but … it requires an interactive platform. Considering the reward is cell rejuvenating, mind bending, life enhancing design – it should not surprise that the process involves more than pen,paper and a book. It requires that we not only stimulate inspiration and imagination, but also subjective time lines and our priming potential. It needs to be interactive.

The need for such interactivity in the process can be resolved with a workshop. For those who may not want to attend one, there have been many clues along the way to at least help achieve more than a decorators make-over.

I am currently investigating the development of an interactive website, it is challenging as the technology lacks the spontaneity required for sensorial triggers…. so far.

For architects, designers and other professionals wishing to learn more about this work from a teaching perspective, and to work with clients – there will be specialist courses. You can see my website for details and dates.

General workshops will be taking place throughout 2014

The larger body of research from which this small book is distilled, will be published in autumn 2014.

I hope you have enjoyed the journey.

I wish you a smile in your mind.

Contact details
www.theroomthatchangesyourbrain.com

Bibliography

Damasio, Antonio, *The feeling of what happens; Decarte's error*

Gribben, John, *In search of Schroedinger's cat*

Kandel, Erik, *In search of memory;*

Kandel, Erik & Schwartz, James & Jessel, Thomas, *Principles of neuroscience,*

Kandel, Erik & Squire, Larry, *Memory- from mind to molecules*

Lakoff, George & Johnson, Mark, *The phlosophy of the flesh*

Langer, Ellen, *Counterclockwise*

Ledoux, Joseph, *The emotional brain*

Merleau-Ponty, Maurice, *Phenomenology of perception The world of perception*

Pert, Candace B, *Molecules of emotion*

Pinker, Steven, *How the mind works; The stuff of thought*

Michio, Kaku, *Parallel worlds; The physics of the impossible*

Ramachandran, V S, *A brief tour of human consciousness; The tell-tale brain*

Sacks, Oliver, *The man who mistook his wife for a hat*

Smolin, Lee, *The trouble with physics*

Thompson, Eric, *Mind in life*

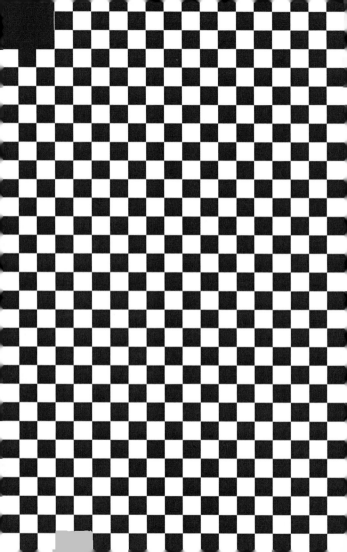